The Door Is Open
Hymns and Tunes for Today's Church

Copyright © 2002 Abingdon Press

All rights reserved.

ISBN-0-687-080746

02 03 04 05 06 07 08 09 10 11 — 10 9 8 7 6 5 4 3 2 1

THE DOOR IS OPEN

Hymns and Tunes for Today's Church

Tunes by
Carlton R. Young

Texts by
Carl P. Daw, Jr.
Ruth Duck
Timothy Dudley-Smith
Colin Gibson
Fred Pratt Green
Fred Kaan
Shirley Erena Murray
Thomas H. Troeger
Brian Wren

Foreword by Don E. Saliers

Abingdon Press
Nashville

Foreword

Having known and worked with Carlton Young for nearly thirty years, I am never surprised by his musical and theological creativity. A prolific composer and arranger, and the only musician to edit two twentieth-century hymnals for the same denominational family, "Sam" is a true servant of the Church's sung prayer and prophecy. This collection of fine hymn tunes is evidence of his continuing vitality and vision.

Within brief compass these tunes sound a distinctive voice. Three things are worth special mention. First, the texts he chooses to set are by some of our best Christian poets. Shirley Erena Murray, Thomas Troeger, Brian Wren, and the rest combine deep appreciation of Scripture with a profound perception of human life before God.

Well-crafted melodic lines are a second feature of this collection. The "shape" of these tunes, as Erik Routley would say, fits the contour of the sense of the words. One hears in several of them a Carlton Young signature—often a "blue note" at a crucial point in the line (once a jazzman, always a jazzman). He has a wonderful ear for a truly American sound, the blending of English, European, and African American musical sensibility, and sonic radar for how people sing.

A third feature to listen for is his harmonic colors and unerring rhythmic sense.

But here one also finds that irrepressible, impish side, shown in his text and tune "Synergy." We can use some fun like this parody in show-tune style of our contemporary "church-speak" jargon. Don't be offended; "just delight in the thing" I hear him say.

Beyond the discovery of these musical values and the joy of singing, we enter here into the truths and the mystery that the Church needs to sing. Happy are the poets upon whose lines Carlton Young's musical eyes and ears focus. Above all, sing lustily and with good courage, and, as John Wesley added, sing spiritually.

Don E. Saliers
William R. Cannon Professor of Theology and Worship
Candler School of Theology, Emory University, Atlanta, Georgia

Contents

Welcome, Welcome! The Door Is Open

Welcome, welcome!
The door is open,
there's room for all who come,
the table's laid, the meal prepared,
enough for everyone.

Refrain
This is God's feast, unlike any other,
where the greatest and least
are sister and brother.

Welcome, welcome!
You're not too early,
too late, too well-to-do,
too poor to be an honored guest.
A place is set for you.

Refrain

Welcome, welcome!
Come join the circle.
Enjoy the wine and bread,
and pass them on to foes and friends
till everyone is fed.

Refrain

Welcome, welcome!

WORDS: Thomas H. Troeger (Matt. 22:1-10)
© 2002 Oxford University Press, Inc.

Welcome, Welcome! The Door Is Open

Lyrics (under the music):

1. Wel - come, wel - come! The door is o - pen, there's room for all who come, the
2. Wel - come, wel - come! You're not too ear - ly, too late, too well - to - do, too
3. Wel - come, wel - come! Come join the cir - cle. En - joy the wine and bread, and

A separate flute part is printed on pages 8-9. Note: St. 2, flute tacet until refrain.
**These four measures may be repeated as an extended introduction and interlude between stanzas.*

WORDS: Thomas H. Troeger (Matt. 22:1-10)
MUSIC: Carlton R. Young

WELCOME
456.446 with Refrain

Words © 2002 Oxford University Press, Inc.; music © 2002 Abingdon Press, admin. by The Copyright Co.

ta - ble's laid, the meal pre - pared, e -
poor to be an hon - ored guest. A
pass them on to foes and friends till

nough for ev - ery - one.
place is set for you.
ev - ery - one is fed.

This is God's feast, un - like an - y oth - er,

where the great - est and least   are

Third time to Coda   D.C. al Coda

sis - ter   and broth - er.

Third time to Coda   D.C. al Coda

CODA   repeat ad lib

broth - er.   Wel - come, wel - come!

CODA   repeat ad lib

7

Welcome, Welcome! The Door Is Open

*These four measures may be repeated as an extended introduction and interlude between stanzas.
**Stanza 1, play top line; st. 2, tacet until refrain, then play bottom line; st. 3, play bottom line.

MUSIC: Carlton R. Young

© 2002 Abingdon Press, admin. by The Copyright Co.

8

8
11
ten.,
Refrain
ten.,
14
f
Third time to Coda
D.C. al Coda
16
CODA
repeat ad lib
19
7

Welcome, Welcome! The Door Is Open

(♩. = 60-64)

1. Wel - come, wel - come! The door is
2. Wel - come, wel - come! You're not too
3. Wel - come, wel - come! Come join the

o - pen, there's room for all who come, the
ear - ly, too late, too well - to - do, too
cir - cle. En - joy the wine and bread, and

ta - ble's laid, the meal pre - pared, e -
poor to be an hon - ored guest. A
pass them on to foes and friends till

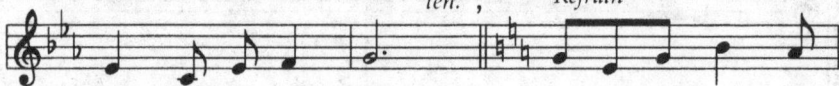

ten. ,   *Refrain*

nough for ev - ery - one.
place is set for you.   This is God's feast, un -
ev - ery - one is fed.

like an - y oth - er,   where the great - est and

| 1, 2 | D.C. |

least are sis - ter and broth - er.

3

repeat ad lib   (⌢)

broth - er.   Wel - come! Wel - come!

WORDS: Thomas H. Troeger (Matt. 22:1-10)
MUSIC: Carlton R. Young

WELCOME
456.446 with Refrain

When We Are Tested

When we are tested and wrestle alone,
famished for bread when the world offers stone,
nourish us, God, by your word and your way,
food that sustains us by night and by day.

When in the desert we cry for relief,
pleading for paths marked by certain belief,
lift us to love you beyond sign and test,
trusting your presence, our only true rest.

When we are tempted to barter our souls,
trading the truth for the power to control,
teach us to worship and praise only you,
seeking your will in the work that we do.

When we have struggled and searched through the night,
sorting and sifting the wrong from the right,
Savior, surround us with circles of care,
angels of healing, of hope, and of prayer.

WORDS: Ruth Duck (based on Luke 4:1-11); inspired by a sermon by Barbara Troxell and
a request by Bonnie Beckonchrist

Unison
(♩ = ca. 100)

When We Are Tested

1. When we are test - ed and wres - tle a - lone,
2. When in the des - ert we cry for re - lief,
3. When we are tempt - ed to bar - ter our souls,
4. When we have strug - gled and searched through the night,

fam - ished for bread when the world of - fers stone,
plead - ing for paths marked by cer - tain be - lief,
trad - ing the truth for the power to con - trol,
sort - ing and sift - ing the wrong from the right,

nour - ish us, God, by your word and your way,
lift us to love you be - yond sign and test,
teach us to wor - ship and praise on - ly you,
Sav - ior, sur - round us with cir - cles of care,

food that sus - tains us by night and by day.
trust - ing your pres - ence, our on - ly true rest.
seek - ing your will in the work that we do.
an - gels of heal - ing, of hope, and of prayer.

WORDS: Ruth Duck (based on Luke 4:1-11); inspired by a sermon by Barbara Troxell and a request by Bonnie Beckonchrist
MUSIC: Carlton R. Young

ANGELS OF HEALING
10 10.10 10

When We Are Tested

($\boldsymbol{\downarrow}$ = ca. 100)

1. When we are test-ed and wres-tle a-lone,
2. When in the des-ert we cry for re-lief,
3. When we are tempt-ed to bar-ter our souls,
4. When we have strug-gled and searched through the night,

fam-ished for bread when the world of-fers stone,
plead-ing for paths marked by cer-tain be-lief,
trad-ing the truth for the power to con-trol,
sort-ing and sift-ing the wrong from the right,

nour-ish us, God, by your word and your way,
lift us to love you be-yond sign and test,
teach us to wor-ship and praise on-ly you,
Sav-ior, sur-round us with cir-cles of care,

[1-3] [4]

food that sus-tains us by night and by day.
trust-ing your pres-ence, our on-ly true rest.
seek-ing your will in the work that we do.
an-gels of heal-ing, of hope, and of prayer.

WORDS: Ruth Duck (based on Luke 4:1-11); inspired by a sermon by
Barbara Troxell and a request by Bonnie Beckonchrist
MUSIC: Carlton R. Young

ANGELS OF HEALING
10 10.10 10

How Deep Our Maker's Grief

How deep our Maker's grief
when love is pushed aside,
and lives impaled by harsh belief
are crushed and crucified.

Tomorrow may explain
the how, and who, and why;
today we drink the cup of pain
and vent our grieving cry.

Let love's lament dissolve
aloofness and despair,
and resurrect our best resolve
to comfort, pray, and care.

The hymn was first written in April, 1993, after the death of
children, women, and men in the Branch Davidian compound in
Waco, Texas. It was revised and shortened in response to the
bombings of the World Trade Center, New York City, and the
Pentagon, Washington, D. C., on September 11, 2001. This version
was first sung at Cannon Chapel, Candler School of Theology,
Emory University, Atlanta, Georgia, September 20, 2001.

WORDS: Brian Wren
© 1996, 2001 Hope Publishing Co.

How Deep Our Maker's Grief

(♩ = 68)   *Unison*

1. How deep our Mak-er's
(2. To-) mor-row may ex-
(3. Let) love's la-ment dis-

grief when love is pushed a - side, and
plain the how, and who, and why; to-
solve a - loof-ness and de-spair, and

lives im-paled by harsh be-lief are crushed and cru-ci-
day we drink the cup of pain and vent our griev-ing
res - ur-rect our best re-solve to com - fort, pray, and

1, 2   **3**   *rit.*

fied.   2. To -
cry.   3. Let
care.

WORDS: Brian Wren
MUSIC: Carlton R. Young

BARBARA
SM

Words © 1996, 2001 Hope Publishing Co.; music © 2002 Abingdon Press, admin. by The Copyright Co.

15

How Deep Our Maker's Grief

(♩ = 68)

1. How deep our Mak-er's grief when love is pushed a-
(2. To -) mor-row may ex - plain the how, and who, and
(3. Let) love's la - ment dis - solve a - loof-ness and de-

side, and lives im-paled by harsh be - lief are
why; to - day we drink the cup of pain and
spair, and res - ur-rect our best re-solve to

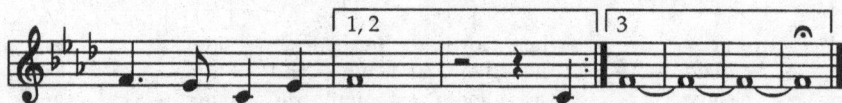

1, 2

crushed and cru - ci - fied. 2. To -
vent our griev-ing cry. 3. Let
com - fort, pray, and

3

care. _____

WORDS: Brian Wren
MUSIC: Carlton R. Young

BARBARA
SM

Words © 1996, 2001 Hope Publishing Co.; music © 2002 Abingdon Press, admin. by The Copyright Co.

16

Carol of Dreams

Dream a dream, a hopeful dream
as children do on Christmas Eve,
imaginings, surprising things
to hold and to believe.

Dream a time this Christmas time
when no one's hungry or afraid;
that weapons go and harvests grow,
that friends are met and made.

Dream a peace, our planet's peace,
the greening of the earth at play,
the holy ground where life is found,
where God has touched the clay.

Dream a gift, the Christmas gift
that changes everything we see:
the shimmering of angel wing,
the Child, the Mystery.

WORDS: Shirley Erena Murray
© 1997 Hope Publishing Co.

Carol of Dreams

Unison
($\downarrow$ = 60)

1. Dream a dream, a hope-ful dream as chil-dren
(2. Dream a) time this Christ-mas time when no one's
(3. Dream a) peace, our plan-et's peace, the green-ing
(4. Dream a) gift, the Christ-mas gift that chang-es

a little faster

do on Christ-mas Eve, i-mag-in-ings, sur-
hun-gry or a-fraid; that weap-ons go and
of the earth at play, the ho-ly ground where
ev-ery-thing we see: the shim-mer-ing of

pris-ing things to hold and to be-
har-vests grow, that friends are met and
life is found, where God has touched the
an-gel wing, the Child, the Mys-ter-

1-3
lieve. 2. Dream a
made. 3. Dream a
clay. 4. Dream a

4

Solo Dream a dream.

y.

WORDS: Shirley Erena Murray
MUSIC: Carlton R. Young

DREAM VISION
78.86

18

Carol of Dreams

(♩ = 60)

a little faster

1. Dream a dream, a hope-ful dream as chil-dren
(2. Dream a) time this Christ-mas time when no one's
(3. Dream a) peace, our plan-et's peace, the green-ing
(4. Dream a) gift, the Christ-mas gift that chang-es

do on Christ-mas Eve, i - mag-in-ings, sur-
hun-gry or a - fraid; that weap-ons go and
of the earth at play, the ho - ly ground where
ev - ery-thing we see: the shim-mer-ing of

pris - ing things to hold and to be -
har - vests grow, that friends are met and
life is found, where God has touched the
an - gel wing, the Child, the Mys - ter -

1-3

lieve. 2. Dream a
made. 3. Dream a
clay. 4. Dream a

4

y.

WORDS: Shirley Erena Murray
MUSIC: Carlton R. Young

DREAM VISION
78.86

Words © 1997 Hope Publishing Co.; music © 2002 Abingdon Press, admin. by The Copyright Co.

A New Day Bids Us Wake

A new day bids us wake
to clear or cloudy weather,
and for each other's sake
restores us to each other:
Remembering God, we say:
This is God's world, God's day.

As all life needs the sun,
which never ceases giving,
even when day is done,
its energy for living:
Forget God though we may,
this is God's world, God's day.

Once more we rise to face
another day's beginning,
to find in God's free grace
forgiveness for our sinning:
Resist God though we may,
this is God's world, God's day.

So now, in solitude,
or met in Christ together,
we praise our living God,
and pray for one another:
Believing, come what may,
this is God's world, God's day.

WORDS: Fred Pratt Green
© 1975 Hope Publishing Co.

20

A New Day Bids Us Wake

Unison

(♩ = 116)

1. A new day bids us wake to clear or cloud-y
(2. As) all life needs the sun, which nev-er ceas-es
(3. Once) more we rise to face an-oth-er day's be-
(4. So) now, in sol-i-tude, or met in Christ to-

weath-er, and for each oth-er's sake re-stores us to each
giv-ing, e-ven when day is done, its en-er-gy for
gin-ning, to find in God's free grace for-give-ness for our
geth-er, we praise our liv-ing God, and pray for one an-

oth-er: Re-mem-b'ring God, we say:
liv-ing: For-get God though we may,
sin-ning: Re-sist God though we may,
oth-er: Be-liev-ing, come what may,

[1-3]   *rit.*   [4]

This is God's world, God's day.   2. As
this is God's world, God's day.   3. Once
this is God's world, God's day.   4. So
this is God's world, God's   day.

WORDS: Fred Pratt Green
MUSIC: Carlton R. Young

GREEN
6 7.6 7.6 6

A New Day Bids Us Wake

(♩ = 116)

1. A new day bids us wake to clear or cloud-y
(2. As) all life needs the sun, which nev-er ceas-es
(3. Once) more we rise to - face an-oth-er day's be -
(4. So) now, in sol - i - tude, or met in Christ to -

weath - er, and for each oth - er's sake re -
giv - ing, e - ven when day is done, its
gin - ning, to find in God's free grace for -
geth - er, we praise our liv - ing God, and

stores us to each oth - er: Re - mem-b'ring God, we say:
en - er - gy for liv - ing: For - get God though we may,
give - ness for our sin - ning: Re - sist God though we may,
pray for one an - oth - er: Be - liev - ing, come what may,

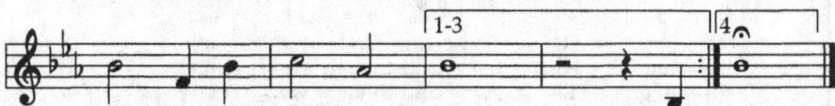

1-3

This is God's world, God's day.
this is God's world, God's day.
this is God's world, God's day.
this is God's world, God's

4

2. As
3. Once
4. So
day.

WORDS: Fred Pratt Green
MUSIC: Carlton R. Young

GREEN
6 7.6 7.6 6

The Ho-Hum Hymn

Snap us out of it, Lord, we are listless and bored,
we have practiced too much of the same;
yes, we've hymned and we've hawed, we have praised and adored
till there's nothing much left but your name.
Ho-hum, ho-hum, keep those ho-hums away;
caring, daring, life more abundant,
new life every day. Hey! Hey!

We are frozen and still, hardly notice the chill,
it must surely be time for a thaw;
we are good, we are nice, but we're stuck in the ice
half a hundred miles out from the shore.
Snow-white, frostbite, keep those winters away;
seeing, being, life more abundant,
new life every day. Hey! Hey!

We're your comfortable sheep, with our minds half-asleep,
all our pasture is turning to hay;
an occasional bleat, or a stamp of the feet,
is as much as we dare when we pray.
Hum-drum, hum-drum, keep those hum-drums away;
yearning, learning, life more abundant,
new life every day. Hey! Hey!

Wake us up from our trance, call us into the dance
of the riotous Spirit of God;
there's no sitting it out while the world leaps about —
and just give us a tap if we nod.
Ho-hum, ho-hum, keep those ho-hums away;
filling, spilling, life more abundant,
new life every day. Hey! Hey!

WORDS: Colin Gibson
© 1996 Hope Publishing Co.

The Ho-Hum Hymn

noth-ing much left but your name.
hun-dred miles out from the shore.
much as we dare when we pray.
give us a tap if we nod.

Ho - hum, ho - hum, keep those ho - hums a - way;
Snow white, frost - bite, keep those win - ters a - way;
Hum - drum, hum - drum, keep those hum-drums a - way;
Ho - hum, ho - hum, keep those ho - hums a - way;

car - ing, dar - ing,
see - ing, be - ing,
yearn - ing, learn - ing, life more a - bun - dant, new
fill - ing, spill - ing,

life ev-ery day. Hey! Hey! 2. We are
3. We're your
4. Wake us

Hey!

25

The Ho-Hum Hymn

(♩ = 66)

1. Snap us out of it, Lord, we are list - less and
(2. We are) fro - zen and still, hard - ly no - tice the
(3. We're your) comf' - ta - ble sheep, with our minds half - a -
(4. Wake us) up from our trance, call us in - to the

bored, we have prac - ticed too much of the
chill, it must sure - ly be time for a
sleep, all our pas - ture is turn - ing to
dance, of the ri - ot - ous Spir - it of

same; yes, we've hymned and we've hawed, we have
thaw; we are good, we are nice, but we're
hay; an oc - ca - sion - al bleat, or a
God; there's no sit - ting it out while the

praised and a - dored till there's noth - ing much left but your
stuck in the ice, half a hun - dred miles out from the
stamp of the feet, is as much as we dare when we
world leaps a - bout — and just give us a tap if we

name. Ho - hum, ho - hum,
shore. Snow white, frost - bite,
pray. Hum - drum, hum - drum,
nod. Ho - hum, ho - hum,

WORDS: Colin Gibson
MUSIC: Carlton R. Young
HO-HUM
12 9.12 9.10 9.7
Words © 1996 Hope Publishing Co.; music © 1996 Abingdon Press, admin. by The Copyright Co.

26

keep those ho - hums a - way;   car - ing,
keep those win - ters a - way;   see - ing,
keep those hum-drums a - way;   yearn - ing,
keep those ho - hums a - way;   fill - ing,

dar - ing, ⎫
be - ing, ⎬   life   more a - bun - dant, new
learn - ing,⎪
spill - ing,⎭

life   ev - ery day.   Hey! Hey! ⎰ 2. We are
                                      ⎱ 3. We're your
                                        4. Wake us

                                              Hey!

Christ the Way of Life Possess Me

Christ the Way of life possess me,
lift my heart to love and praise;
guide and keep, sustain and bless me,
all my days.

Well of life, forever flowing,
make my barren soul and bare
like a watered garden growing
fresh and fair.

May the Tree of life in splendor
from its leafy boughs impart
grace divine and healing tender,
strength of heart.

Path of life before me shining,
let me come when earth is past,
sorrow, self and sin resigning,
home at last.

WORDS: Timothy Dudley-Smith (based on four images from the Book of Proverbs)
© 1988 Hope Publishing Co.

Christ the Way of Life Possess Me

1. Christ the Way of life pos-sess me, lift my heart to love and praise; guide and keep, sus-tain and bless me, all my days.
2. Well of life, for-ev-er flow-ing, make my bar-ren soul and bare like a wa-tered gar-den grow-ing fresh and fair.
3. May the Tree of life in splen-dor from its leaf-y boughs im-part grace di-vine and heal-ing ten-der, strength of heart.
4. Path of life be-fore me shin-ing, let me come when earth is past, sor-row, self and sin re-sign-ing, home at last.

WORDS: Timothy Dudley-Smith (based on four images from the Book of Proverbs)   NEW FOREST
MUSIC: Carlton R. Young   87.83

Words © 1988 Hope Publishing Co.; music © 1996 Abingdon Press, admin. by The Copyright Co.

Duplication without permission is strictly prohibited.

29

Christ the Way of Life Possess Me

($\downarrow$ = 88)

1. Christ the Way of life pos - sess me,
2. Well of life, for - ev - er flow - ing,
3. May the Tree of life in splen - dor
4. Path of life be - fore me shin - ing,

lift my heart to love and praise; guide and keep, sus -
make my bar - ren soul and bare like a wa - tered
from its leaf - y boughs im - part grace di - vine and
let me come when earth is past, sor - row, self and

tain and bless me, all my days.
gar - den grow - ing fresh and fair.
heal - ing ten - der, strength of heart.
sin re - sign - ing, home at last.

WORDS: Timothy Dudley-Smith (based on four images from the Book of Proverbs)
MUSIC: Carlton R. Young

NEW FOREST
87.83

Words © 1988 Hope Publishing Co.; music © 1996 Abingdon Press, admin. by The Copyright Co.

Duplication without permission is strictly prohibited.

How Privileged We Are Who Worship in This Place

How privileged we are who worship in this place!
May no distinctions mar the miracle of grace.
Here shall a stranger be at home,
for God it is who bids us come.

Rejoice in every art we put to sacred use,
that lifts the leaden heart, and beautifies God's House.
May all we see and do declare
what kind of God we worship here.

Rejoice in music's power to lend the spirit wings,
in that inspiring hour when faith with fervor sings.
May love revealed, convincing all,
turn formal praise to festival.

Rejoice in words that bear the weight of God's command,
that we who read or hear may heed and understand.
Christ's glorious gospel we receive
with fresh surprise and dare believe.

Thus, mighty Spirit, raise our worship from the ground,
to heights from which we gaze this needy world around.
Returning, may our witness prove
how Christ is teaching us to love.

WORDS: Fred Pratt Green
© 1989 Hope Publishing Co.

Tune commissioned for the 20th Anniversary of Cannon Chapel,
Candler School of Theology, Emory University, Atlanta, Georgia
September 20-21, 2001

How Privileged We Are Who Worship in This Place

Unison

($\quad$ = 86)

1. How priv - i - leged we are who wor - ship in this place! May no dis - tinc - tions mar the mir - a - cle of grace. Here

(2. Re -) joice in ev - ery art we put to sa - cred use, that lifts the lead - en heart, and beau - ti - fies God's House. May

(3. Re -) joice in mu - sic's power to lend the spir - it wings, in that in - spir - ing hour when faith with fer - vor sings. May

(4. Re -) joice in words that bear the weight of God's com - mand, that we who read or hear may heed and un - der - stand. Christ's

(5. Thus,) might - y Spir - it, raise our wor - ship from the ground, to heights from which we gaze this need - y world a - round. Re -

WORDS: Fred Pratt Green
MUSIC: Carlton R. Young

HOLTKAMP
12 12.8 8

32

shall a strang-er be at home, for
all we see and do de - clare what
love re-vealed, con - vinc - ing all, turn
glo - rious gos - pel we re - ceive with
turn - ing, may our wit - ness prove how

God it is who bids us
kind of God we wor - ship
for - mal praise to fes - ti -
fresh sur - prise and dare be -
Christ is teach - ing

come. 2. Re -
here. 3. Re -
val. 4. Re -
lieve. 5. Thus,

us   to   love.

33

*Tune commissioned for the 20th Anniversary of Cannon Chapel,
Candler School of Theology, Emory University, Atlanta, Georgia
September 20-21, 2001*

How Privileged We Are Who Worship in This Place

(♩ = 86)

1. How priv - i - leged we are who wor - ship in this
(2. Re -) joice in ev - ery art we put to sa - cred
(3. Re -) joice in mu - sic's power to lend the spir - it
(4. Re -) joice in words that bear the weight of God's com -
(5. Thus,) might - y Spir - it, raise our wor - ship from the

place! May no dis - tinc-tions mar the mir - a - cle of
use, that lifts the lead - en heart, and beau - ti - fies God's
wings, in that in - spir - ing hour when faith with fer - vor
mand, that we who read or hear may heed and un - der -
ground, to heights from which we gaze this need - y world a -

grace. Here shall a strang - er be at home, for
House. May all we see and do de - clare what
sings. May love re-vealed, con - vinc - ing all, turn
stand. Christ's glo - rious gos - pel we re - ceive with
round. Re - turn - ing, may our wit - ness prove how

|1-4| |5 rit.|

God it is who bids us come. 2. Re -
kind of God we wor - ship here. 3. Re -
for - mal praise to fes - ti - val. 4. Re -
fresh sur - prise and dare be - lieve. 5. Thus,
Christ is teach-ing   us to love.

WORDS: Fred Pratt Green
MUSIC: Carlton R. Young

HOLTKAMP
12 12.8 8

Words © 1989 Hope Publishing Co.; music © 2002 Abingdon Press, admin. by The Copyright Co.

34

Let Hope and Sorrow Now Unite

Let hope and sorrow now unite
to consecrate life's ending.
And praise good friends now gone from sight,
though grief and loss are rending.
The story in a well-loved face,
the years and days our thoughts retrace,
are treasures worth defending.

With faith, or doubt, or open mind
we whisper life's great question.
The ebb and flow of space and time
surpass our small perception;
yet knowledge grows with joyful gains
and finds out wonders far more strange
than hopes of resurrection.

Be glad for life, in age or youth:
Its worth is past conceiving.
And stand by justice, love, and truth
as patterns for believing.
Give thanks for all each person gives —
if faith comes true, and Jesus lives,
there'll be an end to grieving.

WORDS: Brian Wren
© 1983 Hope Publishing Co.

Let Hope and Sorrow Now Unite

Unison

($\quad$ = 92)

1. Let hope and sor - row now u - nite to
2. With faith, or doubt, or o - pen mind we
3. Be glad for life, in age or youth: Its

con - se - crate life's end - ing. And praise good friends now
whis - per life's great ques - tion. The ebb and flow of
worth is past con - ceiv - ing. And stand by jus - tice,

gone from sight, though grief and loss are
space and time sur - pass our small per -
love, and truth as pat - terns for be -

WORDS: Brian Wren
MUSIC: Carlton R. Young

HOPE
87.87.88.7

rend - ing. The sto - ry in a
cep - tion; yet knowl - edge grows with
liev - ing. Give thanks for all each

well - loved face, the years and days our
joy - ful gains and finds out won - ders
per - son gives — if faith comes true, and

thoughts re - trace, are trea - sures worth de - fend - ing.
far more strange than hopes of res - ur - rec - tion.
Je - sus lives, there'll be an end to griev - ing.

*A♮ on stanza 3.

Let Hope and Sorrow Now Unite

(♩ = 92)

1. Let hope and sor - row now u - nite to
2. With faith, or doubt, or o - pen mind we
3. Be glad for life, in age or youth: Its

con - se - crate life's end - ing. And praise good friends now
whis - per life's great ques - tion. The ebb and flow of
worth is past con - ceiv - ing. And stand by jus - tice,

gone from sight, though grief and loss are rend - ing. The
space and time sur - pass our small per - cep - tion; yet
love, and truth as pat - terns for be - liev - ing. Give

sto - ry in a well-loved face, the years and days our
knowl-edge grows with joy - ful gains and finds out won - ders
thanks for all each per - son gives — if faith comes true, and

thoughts re - trace, are trea - sures worth de - fend - ing.
far more strange than hopes of res - ur - rec - tion.
Je - sus lives, there'll be an end to griev - ing.

WORDS: Brian Wren
MUSIC: Carlton R. Young

HOPE
87.87.88.7

Words © 1983 Hope Publishing Co.; music © 1992 Abingdon Press, admin. by The Copyright Co.

For All Who Have Enriched Our Lives

For all who have enriched our lives,
whom we have loved and known,
for saints alive among us still
by whom our faith is honed,
we thank you, God, who came and comes
through women, children, men,
to share the highs and lows of life:
God-for-us, now as then.

For all who with disarming love
have led us to explore
the risk of reasoning and doubt,
new realms not known before,
we thank you, God, who came and comes
to free us from our past,
from ghettos of a rigid mind,
from truths unfit to last.

For all whose laughter has unnerved
tradition gone awry,
who with incisive gentleness
pursue each human "why?"
we thank you, God, who came and comes
to those who probe and ask,
who seek to know the mind of Christ,
and take the church to task.

Now for each other and ourselves
we pray that, healed of fear,
we may re-live the love of Christ,
prepared in hope to err.
Then leave us, God, who comes and goes,
in humanness to grow,
to care for people, tend the earth
—the only earth we know!

WORDS: Fred Kaan
© 1996 Hope Publishing Co.

For All Who Have Enriched Our Lives

(♩ = 98)

1. For all who have en - riched our lives, whom
2. For all who with dis - arm - ing love have
3. For all whose laugh - ter has un - nerved tra -
4. Now for each oth - er and our - selves we

we have loved and known, for saints a - live a -
led us to ex - plore the risk of rea - son -
di - tion gone a - wry, who with in - ci - sive
pray that, healed of fear, we may re - live the

mong us still by whom our faith is
ing and doubt, new realms not known be -
gen - tle - ness pur - sue each hu - man
love of Christ, pre - pared in hope to

WORDS: Fred Kaan
MUSIC: Carlton R. Young

NASHVILLE
CMD

Words © 1996 Hope Publishing Co.; music © 1996 Abingdon Press, admin. by The Copyright Co.

40

honed, we thank you, God, who came and comes through
fore, we thank you, God, who came and comes to
"why?" we thank you, God, who came and comes to
err. Then leave us, God, who comes and goes, in

wom - en, chil - dren, men, to share the highs and
free us from our past, from ghet - tos of a
those who probe and ask, who seek to know the
hu - man - ness to grow, to care for peo - ple,

lows of life: God - for - us, now as then.
rig - id mind, from truths un - fit to last.
mind of Christ, and take the church to task.
tend the earth — the on - ly earth we know!

*A♮ on stanza 3.

41

For All Who Have Enriched Our Lives

($\quad$ = 98)

1. For all who have en - riched our lives, whom
2. For all who with dis - arm - ing love have
3. For all whose laugh - ter has un - nerved tra -
4. Now for each oth - er and our - selves we

we have loved and known, for saints a - live a -
led us to ex - plore the risk of rea - son -
di - tion gone a - wry, who with in - ci - sive
pray that, healed of fear, we may re - live the

mong us still by whom our faith is
ing and doubt, new realms not known be -
gen - tle - ness pur - sue each hu - man
love of Christ, pre - pared in hope to

honed, we thank you, God, who came and comes through
fore, we thank you, God, who came and comes to
"why?" we thank you, God, who came and comes to
err. Then leave us, God, who comes and goes, in

wom - en, chil - dren, men, to share the highs and
free us from our past, from ghet - tos of a
those who probe and ask, who seek to know the
hu - man - ness to grow, to care for peo - ple,

lows of life: God - for - us, now as then.
rig - id mind, from truths un - fit to last.
mind of Christ, and take the church to task.
tend the earth — the on - ly earth we know!

WORDS: Fred Kaan
MUSIC: Carlton R. Young

NASHVILLE
CMD

Words © 1996 Hope Publishing Co.; music © 1996 Abingdon Press, admin. by The Copyright Co.

42

Let the Truth Shine in Our Speaking

Let the truth shine in our speaking
as the sun in fields by day,
as the pure and slantless streaming
of the noon's revealing ray,
washing earth in heaven's brightness
with the light from straight above,
then we shall be faithful neighbors
linked by Christ's deceitless love.

When we wound or grieve each other
let us name the wrong that's done
never bearing hurt and anger
past the setting of the sun.
For our sin is in our silence,
in the storm that never comes,
or that afterward still lingers
sounding yet its grumbling drums.

As the vesperal light is falling
and the air is cooling down,
as we smell the pines and cedars
and the breathings of the ground,
let Christ's richer mystic fragrance
rise from hearts this day redeemed,
when we spoke the truth as neighbors
while the sunlight brightly streamed.

WORDS: Thomas H. Troeger, from *Borrowed Light*
© 1994 Oxford University Press, Inc.

Commissioned for the Institute of Church Music, the University of Iowa, February 14-16, 2002, in memory of Frederick T. Rahn, 1912-2001

Let the Truth Shine in Our Speaking

Unison

($\quad$ = 82-86)

1. Let the truth shine in our speak-ing as the sun in
2. When we wound or grieve each oth - er let us name the
3. As the ves - peral light is fall - ing and the air is

fields by day, as the pure and slant - less stream-ing
wrong that's done nev - er bear - ing hurt and an - ger
cool - ing down, as we smell the pines and ce - dars

of the noon's re - veal - ing ray, wash - ing earth in
past the set - ting of the sun. For our sin is
and the breath-ings of the ground, let Christ's rich - er

WORDS: Thomas H. Troeger (Ephesians 4:25–5:2)   RAHN
MUSIC: Carlton R. Young   87.87 D

heav - en's bright - ness with the light from
in our si - lence, in the storm that
mys - tic fra - grance rise from hearts this

straight a - bove, then we shall be faith - ful neigh-bors
nev - er comes, or that af - ter - ward still lin - gers
day re-deemed, when we spoke the truth as neigh-bors

1, 2

linked by Christ's de - ceit - less love.
sound - ing yet its grum - bling drums.

3 *rit.* , *rit.*

while the sun-light bright - ly streamed._____

3

rit.

_____ , *rit.*

45

Commissioned for the Institute of Church Music, the University of Iowa, February 14-16, 2002,
in memory of Frederick T. Rahn, 1912-2001

Let the Truth Shine in Our Speaking

1. Let the truth shine in our speak-ing as the sun in
2. When we wound or grieve each oth-er let us name the
3. As the ves-peral light is fall-ing and the air is

fields by day, as the pure and slant-less stream-ing
wrong that's done nev-er bear-ing hurt and an-ger
cool-ing down, as we smell the pines and ce-dars

of the noon's re-veal-ing ray, wash-ing earth in heav-en's bright-ness
past the set-ting of the sun. For our sin is in our si-lence,
and the breath-ings of the ground, let Christ's rich-er mys-tic fra-grance

with the light from straight a-bove, then we shall be
in the storm that nev-er comes, or that af-ter-
rise from hearts this day re-deemed, when we spoke the

1, 2

faith-ful neigh-bors linked by Christ's de-ceit-less love.
ward still lin-gers sound-ing yet its grum-bling drums.
truth as neigh-bors

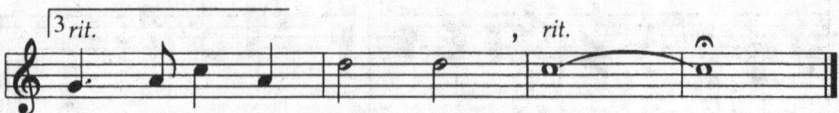

3 *rit.*   , *rit.*

while the sun-light bright-ly streamed.____

WORDS: Thomas H. Troeger (Ephesians 4:25–5:2)   RAHN
MUSIC: Carlton R. Young   87.87 D

46

God of Grace and God of Laughter

God of grace and God of laughter,
singing worlds from nought to be —
sun and stars and all thereafter
joined in cosmic harmony:
give us songs of joy and wonder,
music making hearts rejoice;
let our praises swell like thunder,
echoing our Maker's voice.

When our lives are torn by sadness,
heal our wounds with tuneful balm;
when all seems discordant madness,
help us find a measured calm.
Steady us with music's anchor
when the storms of life increase;
in the midst of hurt and rancor,
make us instruments of peace.

Turn our sighing into singing,
music born of hope restored;
set our souls and voices ringing;
tune our hearts in true accord,
till we form a mighty chorus
joining angel choirs above,
with all those who went before us,
in eternal hymns of love.

WORDS: Carl P. Daw, Jr. (Job 38:7; Isaiah 35:10)

For my friend and colleague, Hugh T. McElrath

God of Grace and God of Laughter

Gracefully (♩ = 72-74)

1. God of grace and God of laugh-ter, sing-ing
2. When our lives are torn by sad-ness, heal our
3. Turn our sigh - ing in - to sing - ing, mu - sic

worlds from nought to be — sun and
wounds with tune - ful balm; when all
born of hope re - stored; set our

*A separate flute part is printed on page 51.
**For learning purposes, consider the following: Stanza 1 - solo; stanza 2 - choir; stanza 3 - congregation

WORDS: Carl P. Daw, Jr. (Job 38:7; Isaiah 35:10)
MUSIC: Carlton R. Young

OCTOGENARIAN
87.87 D

stars and all there - af - ter joined in
seems dis - cor - dant mad - ness, help us
souls and voic - es ring - ing; tune our

(Em) (C/E) (D) (Bm/D)
Fm Db/F Eb Cm/Eb

cos - mic har - mo - ny: give us songs of joy and
find a mea-sured calm. Stea-dy us with mu-sic's
hearts in true ac - cord, till we form a might-y

(C) (G/B) (Bm) (Em) (G)
Db Ab/C Cm Fm Ab

+Fl.

won - der, mu - sic mak - ing hearts re - joice; let our
an - chor when the storms of life in - crease; in the
cho - rus join - ing an - gel choirs a - bove, with all

(D) (G) (C) (C/A) (D) (D/F#)
Eb Ab Db Db/Bb Eb Eb/G

49

prais - es swell like thun - der, e - cho-
midst of hurt and ran - cor, make us
those who went be - fore us, in e -

(G)   (G/C)   (D)   (G)
Ab   Ab/Db   Eb   Ab

-Fl.

1, 2   3

ing our Mak - er's voice.
in - stru-ments of peace.
ter - nal hymns of love.

1, 2   3

(Am)   (Em/B) (Bm) (Em)   (Em)
Bbm   Fm/C   Cm   Fm   Fm

+Fl.   +Fl.

rit.

(E)   (C)   (Am)   (E)
Eb   Db   Bbm   F

rit.

50

God of Grace and God of Laughter

Flute

MUSIC: Carlton R. Young

© 2002 Abingdon Press, admin. by The Copyright Co.

Duplication without permission is strictly prohibited.

For my friend and colleague, Hugh T. McElrath

God of Grace and God of Laughter

Gracefully (♩ = 72-74)

1. God of grace and God of laugh-ter, sing-ing
2. When our lives are torn by sad-ness, heal our
3. Turn our sigh-ing in-to sing-ing, mu-sic

worlds from nought to be — sun and
wounds with tune-ful balm; when all
born of hope re-stored; set our

stars and all there-af-ter joined in cos-mic har-mo-
seems dis-cor-dant mad-ness, help us find a mea-sured
souls and voic-es ring-ing; tune our hearts in true ac-

ny: give us songs of joy and won-der, mu-sic
calm. Stea-dy us with mu-sic's an-chor when the
cord, till we form a might-y cho-rus join-ing

mak-ing hearts re-joice; let our prais-es swell like
storms of life in-crease; in the midst of hurt and
an-gel choirs a-bove, with all those who went be-

thun-der, e-cho-ing our Mak-er's voice.
ran-cor, make us in-stru-ments of peace.
fore us, in e-ter-nal hymns of love.

WORDS: Carl P. Daw, Jr. (Job 38:7; Isaiah 35:10)
MUSIC: Carlton R. Young

OCTOGENARIAN
87.87 D

52

Original Blessing

God was in Christ
and in that frame,
a human child,
God truly came:

In us is held
all that God is —
the will to good,
the well of peace,

the spark to fire
the shape of stars,
the shout of joy
and passion's scars.

That child is born
time after time:
In each of us
God dreams a dream.

Christ is in us
by love conceived,
in struggle born,
in faith believed.

WORDS: Shirley Erena Murray
© 1992 Hope Publishing Co.

Original Blessing

WORDS: Shirley Erena Murray
MUSIC: Carlton R. Young

REBECCA
4 4.4 4

Words © 1992 Hope Publishing Co.; music © 1992 Abingdon Press, admin. by The Copyright Co.

Original Blessing

(♩ = 88-92)

1. God was in Christ and in that
2. In us is held all that God
3. the spark to fire the shape of
4. That child is born time af - ter
5. Christ is in us by love con -

frame, a hu - man child, God
is — the will to good, the
stars, the shout of joy and
time: In each of us God
ceived, in strug - gle born, in

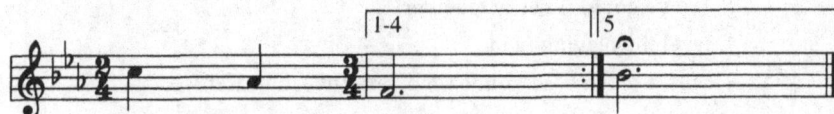

1-4

tru - ly came:
well of peace,
pas - sion's scars.
dreams a dream.

5

faith be - lieved.

WORDS: Shirley Erena Murray
MUSIC: Carlton R. Young

REBECCA
4 4.4 4

Words © 1992 Hope Publishing Co.; music © 1992 Abingdon Press, admin. by The Copyright Co.

Let Us Synergy Together

Let us synergy together,
get on the cutting edge;
with a big picture, hardball, core business, in the ball park,
no-brainer, win-win game!
Let's find the window of opportunity,
empowered, client-focused, value-added, drill down,
with a knowledge base, the best of practice,
benchmark, result driven, mindset, strategic fit.

We've got to synergy together,
level the playing field,
with a touch base, prime time, proactive, mindset,
not out of the loop, game plan.
Within a time frame, and gap analysis,
total quality, and market driven products,
watch the bottom line, staying out of left field,
on fast track, and pushing the envelope.

Let's keep on synerging together,
networking, keep in touch,
as we revisit, with your eye on the ball,
always thinking out of the box!
And keep on synerging, keep synerging,
keep synerging, keep on synerging.
Forever! Synergy!

WORDS: Corporate buzz words
© 2002 Abingdon Press, admin. by The Copyright Co.

Let Us Synergy Together

Let us syn - er - gy *to - geth - er,
syn - er - gy to - geth - er,
syn - er - ging to - geth - er,

Names of leaders, officials, or departments may be substituted, e. g., "with Wesley."

WORDS: Corporate buzz words
MUSIC: Carlton R. Young

SYNERGY
Irr.

© 2002 Abingdon Press, admin. by The Copyright Co.

Duplication without permission is strictly prohibited.

get on the cut - ting edge; ___ with a
lev - el the play - ing field, ___ with a
net - work - ing, keep in touch, ___ as we

Eᵇmaj7   Gm   D/F♯

big pic - ture, hard - ball, core busi - ness, in the ball park,
touch base, ___ prime time, pro - ac - tive, mind - set, not
re - vis - it, with your eye on the ball, al - ways

Fm7   B♭/A♭   E♭/G E♭aug/G   Fm7/A♭   F7/A

Third time to Coda ⊕

no - brain - er, win - win game! Let's find the
out of the loop, game plan. With - in a
think - ing out of the

Third time to Coda ⊕

E♭/B♭   A♭/C   B7   B♭

58

win - dow of op - por - tu - ni - ty, em - powered,
time frame, and gap an - al - y - sis, to - tal

Eb7   Eb7   Db/F   Eb/G

cli - ent-fo - cused, val - ue-add - ed, drill down,   with a
qual - i - ty, and mar - ket driv - en prod - ucts, watch the

Ab   Ab/C   Db   Bbm7

knowl-edge base, the best of prac - tice, bench-mark, re-sult driv - en,
bot - tom line, stay-ing out of left field, on fast track, and

Gm7(b5)   C7   Gm7(b5)   C   C/Bb   Fm/Ab Fm

ging, keep on syn - er -
F/C
F#/C#
G/D
Ab/Eb
ging. For - ev - er!
E
Bb7/F
Eb
shout, clap hands
Syn - er - gy!
Eb
Eb

Let Us Synergy Together

Swing it! (♫ = ♪³♪)

(♩ = ca. 104)

Let us syn - er - gy *to - geth - er,
syn - er - gy to - geth - er,
syn - er-ging to - geth - er,

get on the cut - ting edge; __ with a
lev - el the play - ing field, __ with a
net - work - ing, keep in touch, __ as we

big pic - ture, hard - ball, core busi - ness, in the ball park,
touch base, __ prime time, pro - ac - tive, mind - set, not
re - vis - it, with your eye on the ball, al - ways

Third time to Coda ⊕

no - brain - er, win - win game! Let's find the
out of the loop, game plan. With - in a
think - ing out of the

win - dow of op - por - tu - ni - ty, em - powered,
time frame, and gap an - al - y - sis, to - tal

Names of leaders, officials, or departments may be substituted, e.g., "with Wesley."

WORDS: Corporate buzz words
MUSIC: Carlton R. Young

SYNERGY
Irr.

© 2002 Abingdon Press, admin. by The Copyright Co.

cli - ent-fo - cused, val - ue-add - ed, drill down, with a
qual - i - ty, and mar - ket driv - en prod - ucts, watch the

knowl-edge base, the best of prac -tice, bench-mark, re-sult driv - en,
bot - tom line, stay -ing out of left field, on fast track, and

March on! D.S.

mind - set, stra - te - gic fit. ___ 2. We've got to
push - ing the en - ve - lope. ___ 3. Let's keep on

CODA

box! And keep on syn - er-ging, keep syn - er-ging, keep

grad. cresc.

syn - er ging, keep on syn - er - ging. For -

shout, clap hands

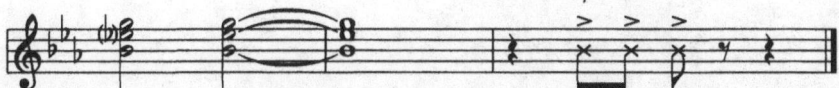

ev - er! ___ Syn - er - gy!

63

More Than We Know

More than we know, God works within us,
more than we trust, mustard seeds grow,
more than we dream, God's possibility,
this is the Gospel of love:

Refrain
For Christ has come, bringing us life,
life in its fullness and joy!
For Christ has come, bringing us life,
life in its fullness and joy!

He is God's eye, changing our focus,
he is the light, flooding our mind,
he is the fire, Spirit and energy
sparking our spirit to shine,

Refrain

He is God's face, smile of the rainbow,
colors of peace, blending us all,
he is the coin, God's new economy,
spending to feed and to save,

Refrain

He is God's heart, tuned to our heartbeat,
he is the air, lifting our wings,
his are the arms stretched out to challenge us,
he is our courage to fly,

Refrain

Joy, joy, joy, joy, joy!

WORDS: Shirley Erena Murray
© 2002 Hope Publishing Co.

More Than We Know

($\quad$ = 126-130)

Hand clapping and percussion

1. More than we know, God works with-in us,
2. He is God's eye, chang-ing our fo - cus,
3. He is God's face, smile of the rain - bow,
4. He is God's heart, tuned to our heart - beat,

more than we trust, mus-tard seeds grow,
he is the light, flood-ing our mind,
col - ors of peace, blend-ing us all,
he is the air, lift - ing our wings,

Repeat first four measures ad lib as introduction and interlude between stanzas.
**A melody instrument may double the voices.*

WORDS: Shirley Erena Murray
MUSIC: Carlton R. Young

TRUE KNOWLEDGE
98.10 7 with Refrain

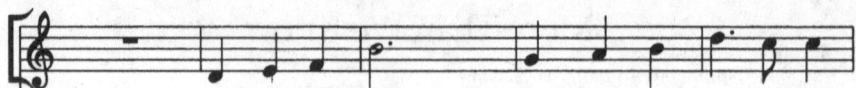

more than we dream,   God's pos - si - bil - i - ty,
he   is   the   fire,   Spir - it   and   en - er - gy
he   is   the   coin,   God's new   e - con - o - my,
his   are the   arms   stretched out   to   chal-lenge us,

Gsus   Dm9   G   Em7   Am7

this   is   the   Gos - pel   of   love: _____
spark-ing   our   spir - it   to   shine, _____
spend-ing   to   feed   and   to   save, _____
he   is   our   cour-age   to   fly, _____

Fm7   G   Dm   Em   Am

Refrain   *add melody instruments*

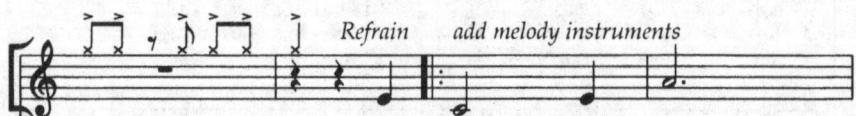

For   Christ   has   come,

Em   N.C.   Am   Dm7

white note
gliss.   ✳

66

bring - ing us life, life in its full - ness and

Dm/G   Em7   Em7   Am7

Repeat ad lib, with
growing intensity.

joy!   For joy!   Joy,

Em   N.C.   Em   Am

joy,   joy,   joy,   joy!

Em   Am   Em   C6,9

fff

More Than We Know

(= 126-130)

1. More than we know, God works with - in us,
2. He is God's eye, chang - ing our fo - cus,
3. He is God's face, smile of the rain - bow,
4. He is God's heart, tuned to our heart - beat,

more than we trust, mus - tard seeds grow,
he is the light, flood - ing our mind,
col - ors of peace, blend - ing us all,
he is the air, lift - ing our wings,

more than we dream, God's pos - si - bil - i - ty,
he is the fire, Spir - it and en - er - gy
he is the coin, God's new e - con - o - my,
his are the arms stretched out to chal - lenge us,

Refrain

this is the Gos - pel of love: ____ For
spark-ing our spir - it to shine, ____
spend-ing to feed and to save, ____
he is our cour-age to fly, ____

Christ has come, bring - ing us life, life in its

1
full - ness and joy!

2
For joy!

WORDS: Shirley Erena Murray
MUSIC: Carlton R. Young

TRUE KNOWLEDGE
98.10 7 with Refrain

Words © 2002 Hope Publishing Co.; music © 2002 Abingdon Press, admin. by The Copyright Co.

Are Shepherds Good?

Are shepherds good?
Some earthly rulers kill the lambs
and terrorize the flock.
Good Shepherd Christ,
kindness of God,
give us shepherds wise,
who rule with love.

Who tends the flock?
Some earthly leaders live in style
and leave the flock unfed.
Good Shepherd Christ,
justice of God,
help us share our goods
and feed your lambs.

Who guards the flock?
Some earthly leaders look away
as wanderers are lost.
Good Shepherd Christ,
send us to seek,
pining while your flock
is incomplete.

Who calls the flock?
All earthly peoples fence apart
the foreign and the found.
Good Shepherd Christ,
life laying down,
gather all your sheep
and make us one.

WORDS: Brian Wren
© 2002 Hope Publishing Co.

Are Shepherds Good?

(♩ = 126)   Solo/soli*

1. Are shep - herds good?   Some
2. Who tends the flock?   Some
3. Who guards the flock?   Some
4. Who calls the flock?   All

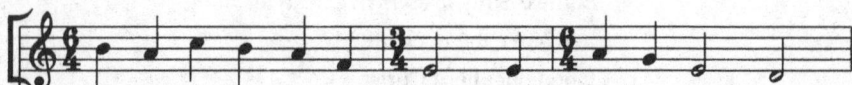

earth-ly rul-ers kill the lambs and ter-ror-ize the
earth-ly lead-ers live in style and leave the flock un -
earth-ly lead-ers look a - way as wan-der-ers are
earth-ly peo-ples fence a - part the for-eign and the

All

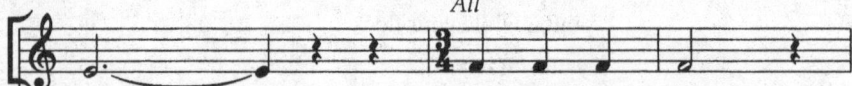

flock.   Good Shep-herd Christ,
fed.   Good Shep-herd Christ,
lost.   Good Shep-herd Christ,
found.   Good Shep-herd Christ,

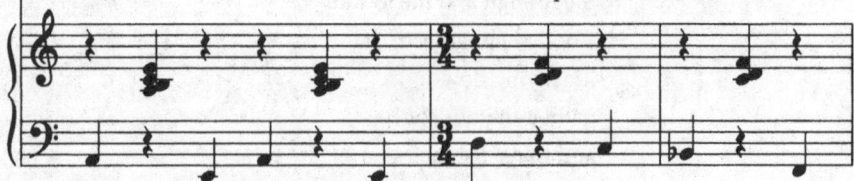

*A melody instrument may double the melody throughout.

WORDS: Brian Wren
MUSIC: Carlton R. Young

WALLER CREEK
486.44.54

kind - ness of God,　　give　us　shep - herds
jus - tice of God,　　help　us　share　our
send us to seek,　　pin　-　ing while　your
life lay - ing down,　gath - er all　your

1-3

wise,　who　rule　　in　　　love.
goods　and　feed　　your　　lambs.
flock　is　in　-　com　-　plete.
sheep　and　make　　us

1-3

4

one.

4

71

Are Shepherds Good?

(♩ = 126)

1. Are shep - herds good? Some earth - ly rul - ers kill the
2. Who tends the flock? Some earth - ly lead - ers live in
3. Who guards the flock? Some earth - ly lead - ers look a -
4. Who calls the flock? All earth - ly peo - ples fence a -

lambs and ter - ror - ize the flock.
style and leave the flock un - fed.
way as wan - der - ers are lost.
part the for - eign and the found.

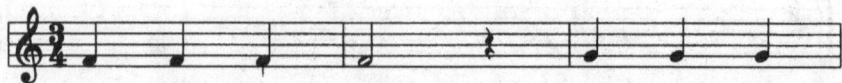

Good Shep - herd Christ, kind - ness of
Good Shep - herd Christ, jus - tice of
Good Shep - herd Christ, send us to
Good Shep - herd Christ, life lay - ing

God, give us shep - herds wise, who
God, help us share our goods and
seek, pin - ing while your flock is
down, gath - er all your sheep and

rule with love.
feed your lambs.
in - com - plete.
make us one.

WORDS: Brian Wren
MUSIC: Carlton R. Young

WALLER CREEK
486.44.54

Metrical Index

SM (66.86)
    BARBARA (15)

CMD (86.86 D)
    NASHVILLE (40)

44.44
    REBECCA (54)

456.446 with Refrain
    WELCOME (5)

486.44.54
    WALLER CREEK (70)

67.67.66
    GREEN (21)

78.86
    DREAM VISION (18)

87.83
    NEW FOREST (29)

87.87 D
    OCTOGENARIAN (48)
    RAHN (44)

87.87.88.7
    HOPE (36)

98.10 7 with Refrain
    TRUE KNOWLEDGE (65)

10 10.10 10
    ANGELS OF HEALING (12)

12 9.12 9.10 9.7
    HO-HUM (24)

12 12.8 8
    HOLTKAMP (32)

Irr.
    SYNERGY (57)

Topical Index

Topical Index (continued)